QUANTUM PATHWAYS

Discovering Your Personal Learning Style

by

Bobbi DePorter
with Mike Hernacki

Learning Forum Publications
Oceanside, California USA

LEARNING FORUM PUBLICATIONS
1725 South Coast Highway
Oceanside, CA 92054-5319 USA
(760) 722-0072
(760) 722-3507 fax
email: info @learningforum.com
www.learningforum.com

Cover design by Kelley Thomas
Illustrations by Ellen Duris

ISBN: 0-945525-22-2

Dedicated to all the very special Learning Forum staff who over the years have contributed so much.

Getting the Most From Your Personality and Learning Style

? *Why is it important to know that people learn in different ways?*

? *How can you categorize people people when each person is an individual?*

? *In taking learning styles tests, what influences your choices?*

? *Do different models measure the same thing?*

Contents

1

Different Ways
of Learning

Have you ever given what you thought were perfectly clear instructions to another, only to find he didn't seem to understand a word you said? Or maybe you've been on the other side of miscommunication, frustrated and lost in a fog of misunderstanding, wondering how you became so dense all of a sudden.

With some people, you never seem able to get your point across. You feel like you're talking to a statue. On the other hand, you probably have some friends who always understand you; they seem to get what you mean almost before you say it. Why is communication so easy with some people and so difficult with others?

Everyone Learns in Different Ways

The answer is so obvious, it's almost a cliché, yet it may surprise you. As you know, each person is different, with unique abilities and gifts. What you may not know, (or may not have thought about), is that each individual also learns in different ways. Thus the manner in which we're taught or spoken to greatly affects what we learn. The key to clear communication and greater learning ability is understanding not only your own learning style, but also the learning styles of others. By knowing how you learn best and by recognizing how others learn, you can discover how to pick up knowledge more easily and communicate more effectively.

The term "learning styles" applies to anything that affects how we learn. This includes the way we take in and process information, plus the ways we think and communicate. Researchers from a number of fields have come up with their own models for identifying different types of learners. Although the names and terminology may vary, most learning style models are surprisingly similar and

Individuals learn in different ways.

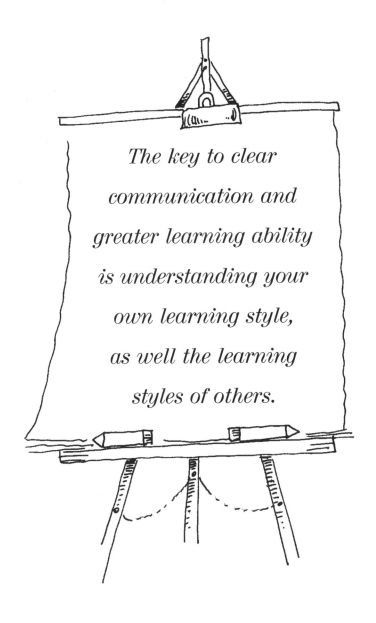

The key to clear communication and greater learning ability is understanding your own learning style, as well the learning styles of others.

many find their roots in the theories of the legendary psychiatrist, Carl Jung.

Research shows that understanding greatly increases when you match your activities with your strongest learning style. According to Rita Dunn, Professor at John Hopkins University in New York, students taught in their preferred learning style have improved attitudes toward learning, increased tolerance for different ways of learning, and increased academic achievement. One of the major benefits of discovering your learning style is that it allows you to take "ownership" of your learning. Once you know your style, you can use it to get the most out of seminars, courses, and the everyday material you must assimilate.

Improving Communication with Style

You can improve communication (and results) when you know how to recognize and tap into the best learning styles of other people. This information will help you improve rapport with your family, friends, and associates; become a better negotiator; enrich your relationships; increase your successes. All this happens because understanding learning styles helps you know yourself and others. It helps you recognize the best, most effective ways to reach all types of people.

In this book, we'll explore several different learning style models. Each one identifies different types of learners and describes some of their habits and abilities. As you read, please keep in mind that these are useful generalizations and do not perfectly describe any one person all the time. Use the categories and labels as guidelines, and remember that people change with their circumstances, sometimes favoring one learning strategy, other times another.

Understanding learning styles helps you know yourself and others.

Your communication will improve, helping you to:

Improve rapport with others

::

Become a better negotiator

::

Enrich your relationships

::

Increase your successes

2

Psycho-Geometric Personality Styles

Take a look at the shapes on the right-hand page. Think of each shape as a person, and in the space provided, write three adjectives that best describe the shape to you. For example, you might describe the Circle as "well-rounded."

Do this now.

Next, choose the shape you feel is most like you—the one that best represents you—and rank it number one. Then rank your next favorite shape number two, and so on, until you have ranked them all, one through five. Your number one shape is your primary shape.

Take time now to complete this exercise so you can get the most out of this chapter.

You've just taken the Psycho-Geometrics personality indicator test, developed by Susan Dellinger, Ph.D. This simple test can tell you a great deal about how your brain works. According to Dr. Dellinger, author of *Psycho-Geometrics, How to Use Geometric Psychology to Influence People,* (Prentice-Hall, Englewood Cliffs, New Jersey, 1989) your personality, experience, education, and the way your brain functions all combine to draw you toward certain shapes. The choices you make and how you perceive the world have a lot to do with whether you favor the left or right hemisphere of your brain.

As you are probably aware, the left and right hemispheres of the brain process information differently. The left hemisphere is logical, sequential, linear, and rational. The right is unordered, intuitive, holistic, and random. Although there is cross-over, your dominant hemisphere determines how you think.

Left-hemisphere thinkers do best in activities that are logical and sequential, and they usually choose the linear shapes. They're more likely to be in a highly structured job

Who are you?

Directions:

- Write 3 adjectives that best describe the shapes.
- Choose your favorite (#1).
- Rank the others (#2 – #5).

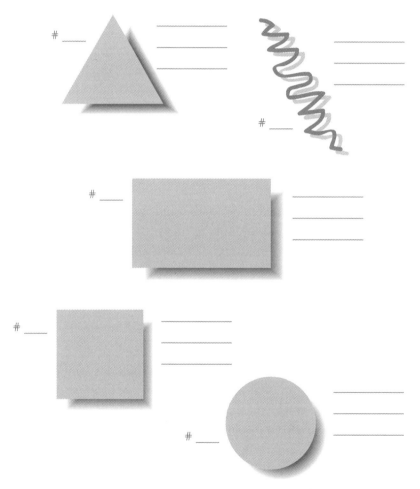

Do this now!

such as an accountant, secretary, or administrator.

Right-hemisphere thinkers tend to be more creative and intuitive, and usually choose the Circle or Squiggle as representing them best. They may pursue careers in the arts, or the "helping professions" like nursing or psychology. Now that you have a basic understanding of Psycho-Geometrics, let's take a look at your test results and discover your learning style.

What Shape Are You?

Your number one shape is an indicator of how you think and behave. Read the description of the shape you chose. Does this person sound familiar? You probably won't match all the attributes of your shape perfectly, but it should paint a pretty good picture of who you are and the ways you learn and communicate.

Triangle Characteristics

Triangles are well-balanced, and their focus is at the top—on goals, career, and moving forward. They have strong leadership skills and are quick to make decisions and take action. They're often athletic and love to compete. Political maneuvering is a strong point with them, and they have the ability to empower others. They're sometimes described as role models.

Other Triangle traits include a driving need to be in control and to be seen as "right." These types are often more interested in their careers than in the work itself, and although they're quick decision-makers, they're likely to choose the course that's in their best interest. They would rather be the team leader than a team player.

Left and right hemispheres of the brain process information differently.

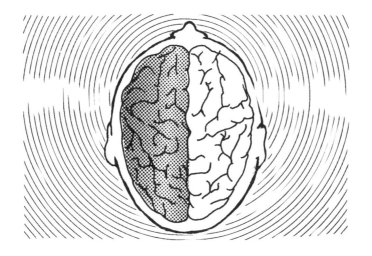

Left-hemisphere thinkers:

- Choose linear shapes

- Choose highly-structured professions

Right-hemisphere thinkers:

- Choose rounded or wavy shapes

- Choose careers in the arts and helping professions

Typical Triangle Jobs
- executive
- manager/supervisor
- entrepreneur
- hospital/school administrator
- politician
- law firm partner
- union organizer
- military officer

Communicating with Triangles

Since Triangles are quick decision-makers and left-hemisphere thinkers, you need to present information to them quickly, clearly, and succinctly. Make sure you have researched all the facts ahead of time. Triangles like information presented logically and sequentially, so avoid jumping around from topic to topic. They like to get to the point quickly.

Triangles often lose emotional control in an argument, so if you can keep your cool you'll have the advantage. If you know you'll be facing an emotional situation with a Triangle, you may want to practice the conversation with a friend ahead of time.

Box Characteristics

The Box is the most structured shape. Box types are hard-working, dedicated, persistent—the ones who get the job done. They're detail-oriented and highly organized. They love factual data, and dislike emotional issues. They're happiest when their lives are controlled and predictable. Following directions and completing projects are their strong points. They're weaker at developing their own plans. Tell them what to do, and they do it.

"Triangles" are well-balanced and focus at the top.

Characteristics:

- :: Strong leadership skills

- :: Quick decision-makers

- :: Athletic

- :: Ability to empower others

- :: Need to control

- :: Left-hemisphere thinkers

Boxes are not strong decision-makers. When unsure of what course to take, they often put off making any decision at all, until forced to do so. They often resist change until they have all the facts and evidence supporting a need for change, and even then may prefer the status quo. They have trouble functioning in an unstructured, disorganized environment. Their highly developed analytical side makes them appear cool and aloof, and their love of details can lead them to be nit-picking perfectionists.

Typical Box Jobs
- accountant
- administrator
- administrative assistant
- doctor
- teacher
- computer programmer
- government worker
- bank teller

Communicating with Boxes
Boxes hate conflict and usually try to avoid it. They're uncomfortable expressing emotion and prefer to solve problems logically and analytically. Boxes will collaborate with others to solve problems as long as the situation remains unemotional and there's plenty of factual data to go on.

When you have to make a proposal to a Box, do your homework. Boxes like to get all the facts, and they'll be armed with their own detailed information. They also prefer to see things in writing and they like reports.

"Boxes" are hard-working, dedicated, and persistent.

Characteristics:

:: Detail-oriented

:: Highly-organized

:: Love factual data

:: Follow directions

:: Complete projects

:: Resist making decisions

:: Left-hemisphere thinkers

Circle Characteristics

Circles are amiable, caring, even-tempered, and well-rounded. They're social "people-persons." Family and friends are important to them. They want to please others and they strive to make sure everyone is happy. They're definitely team players, who dislike conflict and will extend themselves to make things right.

Good interpersonal relations are important to Circles. Their natural empathy, genuine caring, and ability to listen make them the best communicators.

On the downside, Circles sometimes try too hard to please and have trouble saying "no." Others sometimes take advantage of them or manipulate them. They don't like making unpopular decisions or causing upset or strife. At times they spend so much time and energy on others that they neglect their own needs. They also tend to blame themselves when things go wrong.

Typical Circle Jobs

Circles love working with people and helping others. They don't like working alone. Some typical Circle jobs include:
- teacher/trainer
- nurse/doctor
- salesperson
- secretary
- counselor/mental health professional
- human resources
- camp counselor

Communicating with Circles

A Circle with a problem likes to talk about his feelings and can monopolize your time if you let him. Be careful not

"Circles" are amiable, caring, and well-rounded.

Characteristics:

:: Social "people-persons"

:: Pleasers

:: Team players

:: Strong interpersonal skills

:: Good communication

:: Right-hemisphere thinkers

to encourage this behavior.

In conflicts, work for a win/win outcome. Demonstrate how the solution will please others. Help the Circle focus on the problem at hand, rather than on emotions and relationships, and make it clear that the discussion will be kept confidential. Be prepared to deal with hurt feelings. When working with a Circle, help him prioritize his work. Give him a deadline of when it must be done.

Squiggle Characteristics

The Squiggle shape symbolizes creativity. Squiggles are the creative, intuitive, right-hemisphere thinkers. They're likely to experience leaps in thinking, jumping to conclusions or getting a sudden inspiration. Ideas and the big picture interest them more than details. They get excited about new concepts and like to focus on the future. They're naturally expressive and able to motivate others.

However, Squiggles can be disorganized and forgetful of details. Also, they can be difficult for others to understand and their leaps in thought and unstructured manner can frustrate the more structured shapes. The Squiggle doesn't function well in a highly structured environment.

Typical Squiggle Jobs
- strategic planner
- artist/performer/poet
- university professor
- international sales
- inventor
- musician
- promoter/public relations agent

"Squiggles" are creative and intuitive.

Characteristics:

:: Idea generators

:: Conceptualizers

:: Focused on future

:: Expressive

:: Motivators

:: Unstructured

:: Right-hemisphere thinkers

Communicating with Squiggles

Squiggles are powerful, persuasive speakers and often win arguments. However, if you patiently listen to the Squiggle's side first, the Squiggle will be more likely to listen to you. Try to express as much enthusiasm for your ideas as the Squiggle shows for his.

The Squiggle's right-brain leaps in thinking can be difficult for more sequential thinkers to follow, and Squiggles get upset when they're misunderstood. Ask questions and rephrase what the Squiggle has just said to make sure you understand. The Squiggle will feel better knowing you truly do want to understand him and take him seriously.

Rectangles Characteristics

Rectangles represent transition. They're in a temporary state—undergoing major changes in life, questioning their current situation or searching for something new. Rectangles are learning and growing and are excited about upcoming changes in their lives. They're open to new ideas and experiences, but are also easily swayed by any new fad that comes along. They're confused and inconsistent, with personalities that seem to change from day to day, making them very unpredictable. Plus, they're not above some emotional outbursts.

Typical Rectangles Jobs/States
- new bosses
- new graduates
- entrepreneurs
- entry level employees
- performers
- people in mid-life crisis
- new retirees

"Rectangles" are in transition.

Characteristics:

:: Undergoing change

:: Searching for something new

:: Learning and growing

:: Open to new ideas

:: Unpredictable

Communicating with a Rectangle

A Rectangle may change his mind often. He has trouble reaching a decision, and because he's unsure, you're likely to win him over if you present your information clearly, confidently, and convincingly. Find a win/win solution, and finalize everything by putting it in writing. Also, because Rectangles are so unsteady, be sure to offer them lots of support and encouragement.

The Psycho-Geometrics test gives you a good overall picture of how you learn, communicate, and handle the everyday situations that come up in your life. There are, however, many more tests to measure the way you learn.

3

The Gregorc
Model

Anthony Gregorc, professor of curriculum and instruction at the University of Connecticut, has developed a model of brain dominance: the way our brains best process information. His categories are similar to the left-hemisphere/right-hemisphere dominance we mentioned earlier. Gregorc identifies two main ways we process information: concrete and abstract perception; and sequential and random perception.

He combines these two ways of thinking to form four distinct categories: concrete sequential, abstract sequential, concrete random, and abstract random. The sequential thinkers are generally left-hemisphere-dominant, and the random thinkers rely more heavily on the right hemisphere. As with Psycho-Geometrics, knowing what type of thinker you are can help you make the most of your learning abilities and can improve your communication with others whose brains may work differently from yours.

The test on the right hand page was designed by John Parks Le Tellier, an educational consultant and Quantum Learning instructor. This test will help you determine how you process information. Out of each group of words, choose the two that best describe you. Sometimes it helps to go with your first impulse. Be honest in your evaluation of yourself so you can get an accurate picture of your learning style. Remember, there are no right or wrong answers to this test. Do it now.

Let's take a look at your results by marking your answers on the columns on the next page.

Concrete Sequential

These types of thinkers process information in an ordered, step-by-step fashion. Their world is physical and concrete; it consists of the things they can see, touch, hear, taste, and smell. Concrete sequen-

Read each set of words and mark the two that best describe you:

1. a. imaginative
   b. investigative
   c. realistic
   d. analytical

2. a. organized
   b. adaptable
   c. rational
   d. inquisitive

3. a. debating
   b. getting to the point
   c. creating
   d. relating to others

4. a. empathetic
   b. practical
   c. academic
   d. adventurous

5. a. precise
   b. flexible
   c. systematic
   d. inventive

6. a. sharing
   b. orderly
   c. sensible
   d. independent

7. a. competitive
   b. perfectionist
   c. cooperative
   d. logical

8. a. intellectual
   b. sensitive
   c. hard-working
   d. risk-taking

9. a. non-fiction reader
   b. people person
   c. problem-solver
   d. planner

10. a. memorize
    b. associate
    c. think-through
    d. originate

11. a. changer
    b. researcher
    c. spontaneous
    d. wants directions

12. a. communicating
    b. discovering
    c. cautious
    d. reasoning

13. a. challenging
    b. practicing
    c. caring
    d. examining

14. a. completing work
    b. seeing possibilities
    c. gaining ideas
    d. interpreting

15. a. doing
    b. feeling
    c. thinking
    d. experimenting

tial thinkers are detail-oriented and can remember facts, data, and formulas easily. They learn best by doing. They're organizers and perfectionists.

Concrete Random

Like concrete sequentials, concrete random thinkers live in the concrete, physical world. However, their behavior is less structured and they like to experiment. They're often more creative and experience intuitive leaps in thought when searching for a solution. When working on a project, they often get more caught up in the process than in the final outcome, and may lose track of time and miss deadlines. They love to look for alternative ways of doing things and explore new ideas or systems. They follow divergent thought processes.

Abstract Random

Feelings and emotions are primary parts of the abstract random thinkers' world. They need time to reflect on new information before making a decision or forming an opinion. They remember best when information is personalized, and like to see the whole picture before getting into the details to get a clear understanding. They dislike structured environments and are people-oriented. They do well in positions where they can use their creativity.

Abstract Sequential

Abstract sequential thinkers live in a world of theory and thought. They like to analyze information and think in concepts. Their thinking processes are logical, rational, and intellectual, and they like well-organized information and events. Abstract sequential thinkers do well at research, as they are avid

Directions:

- In the columns below, circle the letters of the words you chose for each number.
- Add totals for columns I, II, III, and IV.
- Multiply the total of each column by 4.
- The box with the highest number describes how you most often process information.

1.	C	D	A	B
2.	A	C	B	D
3.	B	A	D	C
4.	B	C	A	D
5.	A	C	B	D
6.	B	C	A	D
7.	B	D	C	A
8.	C	A	B	D
9.	D	A	B	C
10.	A	C	B	D
11.	D	B	C	A
12.	C	D	A	B
13.	B	D	C	A
14.	A	C	D	B
15.	A	C	B	D
	Total	Total	Total	Total
	‾‾‾	‾‾‾	‾‾‾	‾‾‾
	I	II	III	IV

I. ____ x 4 = [＿＿] Concrete Sequential (CS)

II. ____ x 4 = [＿＿] Abstract Sequential (AS)

III. ____ x 4 = [＿＿] Abstract Random (AR)

IV. ____ x 4 = [＿＿] Concrete Random (CR)

readers and find it easy to pinpoint key ideas and information. They're inquisitive and want to understand theories and causes behind effects.

Gregorc's four categories reveal strategies for making learning easy and natural. Take a close look at the descriptions and think of ways you can apply this information to enhance your learning. If you're an abstract random thinker, for example, you may want to get general overviews of new projects or data, then find out how that fits into the bigger picture and how it's valuable to you. Doing this will give the information context and meaning, making it easier for you to delve into the details.

You may have also noticed some similarities between Gregorc's models and Psycho-Geometrics. For example there are some Box characteristics in the concrete sequential thinker—logical, organized, detail-oriented—while the concrete random's people-oriented style is reminiscent of the friendly Circle. As mentioned before, some overlap exists from one learning style theory to another. You'll see how they all fit together at the end of this book. Now let's move on to our final learning style, VAK.

Gregorc Model

The way your brain best processes information.

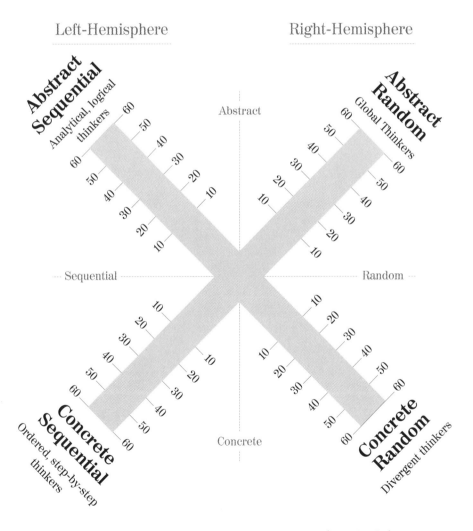

4

VAK:
Seeing, Hearing, Feeling

V AK stands for Visual, Auditory, and Kinesthetic. This is one of the most commonly used tools for evaluating the way people learn, and is cropping up in schools across the country. VAK measures the way we take in information and is built around our senses—what we see, hear and feel. We use all three of these senses to learn, but we usually favor one. Here's a breakdown:

Visual

These learners need to see information, either in writing, or in charts, graphs, pictures, or other visual aids. They can remember what was seen and they will visually reproduce it. Visuals need a big picture and purpose. They use expressions like, "picture this . . ." "looks like . . ." "see . . . " and "focus here . . ."

Auditory

As you can guess, listening and vocalizing are the keys for these types of learners. They learn as if they have a tape recorder in their head, retrieving information exactly as they heard it. They can also mimic tone and pitch. They learn well in lectures and by repeating information and talking to themselves. You'll hear an auditory use these expressions: "sounds like . . ." "rings a bell . . ." "listen . . ." "I hear you loud and clear . . ."

Kinesthetic/Tactile

Hands-on learning works best for Kinesthetics. They learn through experience and actions. They remember feelings and an overall impression of the information. They say things like: "grasp the concept," "get a handle on it," "I'm touched," and "slipped my mind." Tactile learners like to physically manipulate objects in order to grasp the information.

VAK measures the way we take in information.

 Visual learners need to see information

 Auditory learners need to hear and vocalize information

 Kinesthetic / Tactile learners need to have experiences and are referred to as "hands-on" learners

You may already recognize yourself in one of these descriptions. Recognizing preferred learning styles makes it easier for teachers and trainers to reach their students. Plus, it greatly enhances communication and relations. But VAK doesn't stop here. Dawna Markova, learning styles specialist and co-author of *How Your Child is Smart* (Conari Press, Emeryville, Calif. 1992), takes VAK one step further. She stresses that we use all three methods, visual, auditory and kinesthetic, but in different sequences, which in turn correspond to our three different states of mind. She calls these sequences "personal thinking patterns." Here's how that works.

Thinking Patterns

Our personal thinking pattern reflects the way we take information in, store it in our brains, recall it later, and eventually express it. When we learn, information goes first through our conscious mind, then our subconscious, and finally our unconscious mind. According to Markova, we learn best when new information follows this path.

In the conscious state, we organize and evaluate new information. We're alert and focused. The subconscious is the state where we consider information, questioning it, and seeing how it fits with previous learning. In this state we move back and forth from alert to dazed. The unconscious state is where everything sinks in; information is integrated with prior learning, we see the whole situation, and make connections with past experiences. In this state, we experiment and get creative, arranging and rearranging the information in different sequences. We're usually dazed and quiet in this state of mind.

Markova calls VAK the "perceptual channels" that the brain uses to process information, with each channel corre-

When we learn information, it goes through our different states of consciousness.

Conscious State
(alert and focused)

Organize and evaluate new information

Subconscious State
(alert to dazed)

Consider information, question it, and see how it fits withs previous learnings

Unconscious State
(dazed and quiet)

Information sinks in and is integrated; we see the whole picture and make connections sponding to a state. For one person, visual input accesses the conscious state, auditory the subconscious, and kinesthetic the unconscious. However, another learner may do it the other way around, being kinesthetic in the conscious state, auditory in the subconscious, and visual in the unconscious state. There are six different possible combinations— meaning six different ways people learn. We learn best when information is taught in a way that matches our personal thinking pattern.

Personal Thinking Patterns Inventory

(Adapted from *How Your Child Is Smart,* by Dawna Markova)

Directions:

For each question, choose the one answer that's most true. Note the letters in parenthesis following each response. When you've completed the test, transfer these letters to the chart on page 41.

For example, if the response you chose is followed by (U, V), make a mark in both the U and V columns. After you've answered all the questions, total the number of marks in each column. The column with the highest total represents your personal thinking pattern.

Personal Thinking Patterns Inventory

1. **What do you remember most easily?**

   1.1   What's been said, jokes, lyrics, names of people, titles; I memorize by saying something repeatedly. (U, V)

   1.2   What's been seen or read, people's faces, how something looks; I memorize by writing something repeatedly. (Z, Y)

   1.3   What's been done or experienced, the feel or smell of something; I memorize by doing something repeatedly. (X, W)

2. **What do you remember most easily after a movie, TV program or reading?**

   2.1   What the people and the scenes looked like. (Z, Y)

   2.2   What was said or how the music sounded. (U, V)

   2.3   What happened or how the characters felt. (X, W)

3. **What do you remember most easily about people you just met?**

   3.1   What I did with them or how I felt with them. (X, W)

   3.2   How they looked, dressed. (Z, Y)

   3.3   Their names, how they spoke, or what they said. (U, V)

4. **How would you describe your handwriting?**

   4.1   Most of the time my style is neat and legible. (Z, Y)

   4.2   Most of the time my style is difficult to read. (V, X)

   4.3   Most of the time my style is messy. (U, W)

5. **How would you describe your physical needs and skills?**

    5.1   I am constantly in motion, wiggly; I need freedom to move. (X, W)

    5.2   I can sit still easily for long periods. (V, Z)

    5.3   I feel awkward or get easily frustrated when first learning a physical activity. (V, Z)

    5.4   I learn physical skills easily. (X, W)

6. **What's most important when you decide which clothes to wear?**

    6.1   How they feel, how comfortable they are, the texture. (X, W)

    6.2   The colors, how they look on me, how they go together. (Z, Y)

    6.3   An idea of what's me, the brand name, what the clothes say about me. (U, V)

7. **How do you express your feelings?**

    7.1   I'm very private about my feelings. (Z)

    7.2   My feelings seem right beneath the surface. (U, Y)

    7.3   I express feelings easily. (U, W)

    7.4   I express reasons for my feelings easily. (V)

    7.5   It's almost impossible to put my feelings into words. (X)

8. **Under what conditions do you "space out?"**

    8.1   With too much visual detail, being shown something, or questions about what I see. (U, W)

    8.2   With too many words, verbal explanations, or questions about what I have heard. (Y, X)

    8.3   With too many choices of what to do, being touched, or questions about how I feel. (V, Z)

9. How would you describe how you talk?

9.1 My words pour out, in logical order, all the time, without hesitation; I have a very large vocabulary. (U, V)

9.2 I'm self-conscious or shy about speaking in groups. (Y, X)

9.3 I use many metaphors and images. ("It's like cyclone, a blue funnel, a whirling top.") (Z, W)

9.4 I talk mostly about what I did, how I feel, and what's happening. (W)

9.5 I must use my hands or movements to find words. I make hand motions before words. (Y, W)

9.6 I talk in circles, and tend to ask many questions. (Y, X)

10. How would you describe your eye contact?

10.1 I maintain steady, persistent eye contact. (Z, Y)

10.2 I'm "eye shy," and am uncomfortable with eye contact for more than a few seconds. I look away frequently. (U, W)

10.3 I keep steady eye contact, but my eyes blink or twitch if I sustain eye contact. (V, X)

10.4 My eyes glaze over when I listen for too long. (Y, X)

11. What's the hardest for you to take?

11.1 Mean, hurtful words. (Y, X)

11.2 Poking, invasive touch. (V, Z)

11.3 Nasty looks. (U, W)

12. How do you put something together?

12.1 I read the directions and then do it.
Telling me confuses me. (Y)

12.2 I read the directions, ask questions, then
talk to myself as I do it. (Z)

12.3 I work with the pieces, then ask questions if
needed. I never read the directions. (W)

12.4 I work with the pieces, look at the diagram,
then ask questions. (X)

12.5 I have someone tell me, then show me how,
then I try it. (V)

12.6 I have someone tell me how to do it, then I try
it. I only read directions as a last resort. (U)

Identifying Your Thinking Pattern

AKV   (Auditory, Kinesthetic, Visual) "Leaders of the Pack"
These learners are high-energy, take-charge
leaders. They have strong verbal skills and express
themselves well. They love to debate, tell jokes, or
make plays on words. They can remember what
was said word-for-word. They make sounds
constantly, either talking to themselves, whistling,
humming, or singing. They generally do well in
sports and physical activities. They can become
overwhelmed when presented with too much
visual information.

AVK   (Auditory, Visual, Kinesthetic) "Verbal Gymnasts"
AVKs are great talkers, and their verbal ability
makes them appear to be very intelligent. Like
AKVs, they enjoy debating, storytelling, puns and
other verbal feats. They also find it easy to learn
new languages. These learners do well in acade-

Directions:

- For each question, mark the column below that corresponds with the letters in parenthesis that follow your answers.
- If more than one letter is given, mark both columns.
- The column with the most marks represents your personal thinking pattern.

	U	V	W	X	Y	Z
1.						
2.						
3.						
4.						
5.						
6.						
7.						
8.						
9.						
10.						
11.						
12.						
	AKV	AVK	K/TAV	KVA	VKA	VAK

mics but find physical tasks and sports difficult to master. They may shy away from physical contact and have trouble expressing their emotions.

K/TAV (Kinesthetic/Tactile, Auditory, Visual)
"Movers and Groovers"
K/TAVs are physically oriented; they seem to always be moving (kinesthetic) and like to manipulate objects (tactile). Even when they're supposed to be sitting still, they're tapping their feet or fidgeting. They explore the world through touching, doing, and experiencing. Athletics come naturally to them. They're affectionate and respond to touch. They have trouble focusing on visual material.

KVA (Kinesthetic, Visual, Auditory) "Wandering Wonderers"
These learners also find it easy to perform physical tasks and sports, are well coordinated, and have a strong, quiet presence. They have a lot of energy and like to keep moving. They keep to themselves and learn by silently observing others' actions. They may have difficulty verbalizing their feelings and may be overwhelmed by too much talk. They like to look at the big picture and recognize how everything fits together.

VKA (Visual, Kinesthetic, Auditory) "Seers and Feelers"
Seeing and experiencing facilitate learning in VKAs. They easily remember what they have seen or read, and can also learn by imitating someone else's actions. But they may find verbal directions hard to follow. They do their best work in a well-organized environment; they have trouble thinking

Personal thinking patterns reflect how we take in information, store it, recall it, and express it.

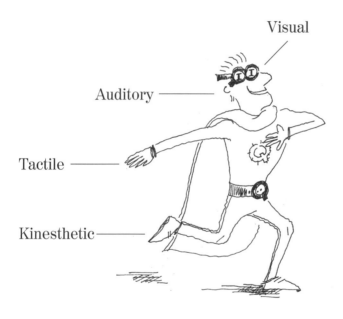

Visual

Auditory

Tactile

Kinesthetic

clearly when their desk is messy. When speaking, they may have difficulty making themselves understood and it can take them a long time to get to the point.

VAK (Visual, Auditory, Kinesthetic) "Show-and-Tellers" VAKs are social, talkative, and friendly. They learn through visual aids like charts, graphs, and pictures, but also do well listening to lectures and can follow spoken directions. They are avid readers, and find it easy to memorize what they read through note-taking and talking to themselves. They may avoid sports and find it hard to learn physical tasks, such as riding a bike; they need lots of practice to master these kinds of activities. They are uncomfortable being touched.

Knowing the sequence of how you learn is as important as knowing your preferred way of processing information. When new information is presented in a way that accesses your conscious state, you'll learn quickly and stay active and alert. If you're VKA, a chart showing company profits will be easy for you to understand, since your conscious state is visual. If, however, someone tells you about the company profits, your mind may become vacant and you may stare into space, since your unconscious state is hooked up with auditory stimulation. Markova's theory goes a long way toward explaining why some people excel in certain classes while others fall behind. It all has to do with matching learning styles.

Knowing your learning sequence is as important as knowing your preferred way of processing information.

AKV – "Leaders of the Pack"

AVK – "Verbal Gymnasts"

K/TAV – "Movers and Groovers"

KVA – "Wandering Wonderers"

VKA – "Seers and Feelers"

VAK – "Show-and-Tellers"

5

Where Do You Fit In?
PUTTING IT ALL TOGETHER

T here are many similarities between the three methods of measuring your learning style reviewed in this book. The chart on the right hand page shows just how each style relates to another.

Circle: right-brain dominant
            concrete random
            VKA/VAK

Squiggle: right-brain dominant
            abstract random
            KVA

Triangle: left-brain dominant
            abstract sequential
            AKV, K/TAV

Box: left-brain dominant
            concrete sequential
            AVK

Rectangle: in transition
            May have many different styles and may
            change from day to day.

Some people are mostly one style; that is, nearly all their preferred learning styles are in the same quadrant on the chart. Others may have one strong style with a tendency toward another style. Still others may be spread out all over the chart. These are usually rectangles!

Whatever your style, the more you know about how you learn, the easier learning can be. Many more methods have been devised for measuring your learning style, personality, behavioral patterns, and so on. All are aimed at increasing self-awareness and cooperation. The Personal

There are many similarities between the methods of measuring learning styles.

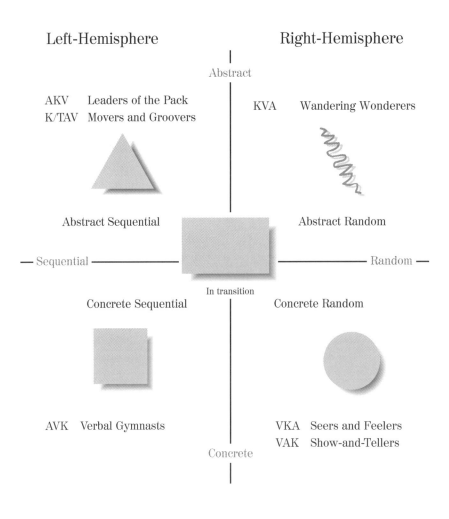

Left-Hemisphere   Right-Hemisphere

Abstract

AKV   Leaders of the Pack   KVA   Wandering Wonderers
K/TAV Movers and Groovers

Abstract Sequential   Abstract Random

— Sequential ——————————————————————————— Random —

In transition

Concrete Sequential   Concrete Random

AVK   Verbal Gymnasts   VKA   Seers and Feelers
                                         VAK   Show-and-Tellers

Concrete

Profile System, sometimes called DISC was developed by Performax Systems International. It's used by many companies to reveal employees' work styles and improve inter-office relations.

To know more about your individual preferences for work or study environments, you may want to take the Learning Styles Inventory and Productivity Environmental Preference Survey, developed by researchers Rita and Kenneth Dunn. Often referred to as the Dunn & Dunn Test, this method helps you design your optimum work environment. It will help you decide such things as:

- Do you need quiet background music or no music?
- Do you do better with dim or bright light?
- Are you better off working with a partner or alone?
- How much structure do you need?
- What is your most productive time of day?

Think about these aspects as you go through your day and be aware of what works best for you. You can accomplish far more when your environment supports your learning style.

Congratulations! You're now equipped with tools for better understanding yourself and others. Not only do you know how you best learn and communicate, but you can recognize the pattern in which you do it. You've also learned strategies for improving your communication with others, and gained some understanding of why you may not always see eye-to-eye with others. When you need to learn new material in optimum time, remember to use your strengths—your strongest learning style. Put this information to work for you and you'll soon begin experiencing fantastic results.

Identifying your learning styles leads to better understanding of yourself and improved communication with others.

Are you:

❏ Mostly one style?

❏ Strong in one style with tendencies toward others?

❏ Nearly equal in all styles?

Celebrate Your Learning!

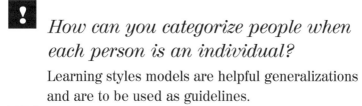

! *Why is it important to know that people learn in different ways?*

Knowing about different learning styles leads to clearer communication, more understanding, and greater learning ability.

! *How can you categorize people when each person is an individual?*

Learning styles models are helpful generalizations and are to be used as guidelines.

! *In taking learning styles tests, what influences your choices?*

Your personality, experiences, education, and the way your brain functions, as well as your current circumstances.

! *Do different models measure the same thing?*

Many vary, including the models used in this book. Psycho-Geometrics is a global model that gives you information on how you learn, communicate, and handle situations. The Gregorc Model tells you how you think and process information. The Personal Thinking Pattern measures your preferred sequence (i.e. VAK) of taking in information, storing it, recalling it, and expressing it.

Since 1981, Learning Forum has produced educational programs for students, educators and business. Its vision is to create a shift in how people learn, so that learning will be joyful, challenging, engaging and meaningful.

Programs and products of Learning Forum—

QUANTUM LEARNING PROGRAMS

Quantum Learning is a comprehensive model of effective learning and teaching. Its programs include: **Quantum Learning for Teachers**, professional development programs for educators providing a proven, research-based approach to the design and delivery of curriculum and the teaching of learning and life skills; **Quantum Learning for Students,** programs that help students master powerful learning and life skills; and **Quantum Learning for Business,** working with companies and organizations to shift training and cultural environments to ones that are both nurturing and effective.

SUPERCAMP

The most innovative and unique program of its kind, SuperCamp incorporates proven, leading edge learning methods that help students succeed through the mastery of academic, social and everyday life skills. Programs are held across the U.S. on prestigious college campuses, as well as internationally, for four age levels: Youth Forum (9-11), Junior Forum (12-13), Senior Forum (14-18), and College Forum (18-24).

SUCCESS PRODUCTS

Learning Forum has brought together a collection of books, video/audio tapes and CD's believed to be the most effective for accelerating growth and learning. The *Quantum Learning Resource Catalog* gives the highlights of best educational methods, along with tips and key points. The Student Success Store focuses on learning and life skills.

For information contact:

LEARNING FORUM
1725 South Coast Highway • Oceanside, CA • 92054-5319 • USA
760.722.0072 • 800.285.3276 • Fax 760.722.3507
email: info@learningforum.com • www.learningforum.com

Great companions to the
Quantum Booklet Series
are the
Learning and Life Skills
Videos and CD s

Quantum Reading *The Power to Read Your Best* • Quantum Strategies *Test-Taking – Simply & Effectively* • Winning the Game of School • Increase your Memory Ten Times • How To " Map" Your Way to Better Grades • Be a Confident Math Solver • Take the Mystery Out of Algebra • The Power of Time Management and Goal-Setting • Build a Winning Attitude • Better Friendships • How to Understand and Be Understood • Money: Earning, Saving and Investing It.

Students will excel with valuable skills usable in any subject!

**Teachers will get through curriculum faster with
deeper meaning and more fun!**

**Call 800.285.3276 or order online
www.learningforumsuccessproducts.com**

Bobbi DePorter is president of Learning Forum, producing programs for students, teachers, schools and organizations across the US and internationally. She began her career in real estate development and ventured to co-found a school for entrepreneurs called the Burklyn Business School. She studied with Dr. Georgi Lozanov from Bulgaria, father of accelerated learning, and applied his methods to the school with great results. Having two children and seeing a need to teach students *how to* learn, she then applied the techniques to a program for teenagers called SuperCamp, which has now helped thousands of students relearn how they learn and reshape how they live their lives. In addition to SuperCamp, Learning Forum produces Quantum Learning for Teachers staff development programs for schools, and Quantum Learning for Business for organizations. Bobbi is also a past president of the International Alliance for Learning.

She is the author of ten books on the subject of learning. *Quantum Learning: Unleashing the Genius in You, Quantum Teaching: Orchestrating Student Success,* and *Quantum Business: Achieving Success through Quantum Learning* are published in the United States, Great Britain, Germany, Slovenia, Brazil, Russia and Indonesia. These books continue to influence the expansion of Quantum Learning programs and draw international interest.

Mike Hernacki, a former teacher, attorney, and stock-broker, has been a freelance writer and marketing consultant since 1979. He is the author of four books: *The Ultimate Secret to Getting Absolutely Everything You want, The Secret to Conquering Fear, The Forgotten Secret to Phenomenal Success,* and *The Secret to Permanent Prosperity.* His books have been translated into six languages and are sold all over the world. He now divides his time between writing and personal success coaching.